STATES

MISSISSIPPI

A MyReportLinks.com Book

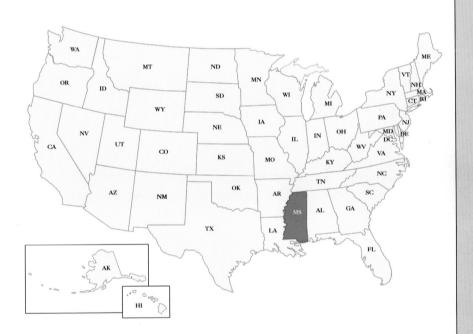

Corinne J. Naden and Rose Blue

MyReportLinks.com Books

an imprint of

 Enslow Publishers, Inc.

Box 398, 40 Industrial Road
Berkeley Heights, NJ 07922
USA

MyReportLinks.com Books, an imprint of Enslow Publishers, Inc. MyReportLinks is a trademark of Enslow Publishers, Inc.

Library of Congress Cataloging-in-Publication Data

Naden, Corinne J.
  Mississippi / Corinne J. Naden and Rose Blue.
    p. cm. — (States)
Summary: Discusses the land and climate, economy, govern-
ment, and history of the state of Mississippi. Includes Internet
links to Web sites. Includes bibliographical references and index.
    ISBN 0-7660-5144-7
    1. Mississippi—Juvenile literature.   [1. Mississippi.]   I.
Blue, Rose. II. Title. III. Series: States (Series : Berkeley Heights,
N.J.)
    F341.3.N33 2003
    976.2—dc21
                              2002153559

10 9 8 7 6 5 4 3 2 1

To Our Readers:
Through the purchase of this book, you and your library gain access to the Report Links that specifically back up this book.

The Publisher will provide access to the Report Links that back up this book and will keep these Report Links up to date on **www.myreportlinks.com** for three years from the book's first publication date.

We have done our best to make sure all Internet addresses in this book were active and appropriate when we went to press. However, the author and the Publisher have no control over, and assume no liability for, the material available on those Internet sites or on other Web sites they may link to.

The usage of the MyReportLinks.com Books Web site is subject to the terms and conditions stated on the Usage Policy Statement on **www.myreportlinks.com**.

A password may be required to access the Report Links that back up this book. The password is found on the bottom of page 4 of this book.

Any comments or suggestions can be sent by e-mail to comments@myreportlinks.com or to the address on the back cover.

Photo Credits: © Corel Corporation, p. 3; © 2001 MCBI, p. 36; © 2001 Mississippi Department of Information Technology Services, p. 32; © 2001 Robesus, Inc., p. 10 (flag); © 2002 Elvis Presley Enterprises, p. 25; © 2003 by the University of Mississippi Medical Center, p. 28; Department of the Interior, p. 38; Enslow Publishers, Inc., pp. 1, 18; Jimmie Rodgers.com, p. 16; Library of Congress, pp. 3 (Constitution), 33; Mississippi.gov/the State of Mississippi, p. 34; MyReportLinks.com Books, p. 4; National Park Service, p. 40; PBS New Perspectives on the West, p. 41; Photo courtesy of the Mississippi Development Authority/Division of Tourism, pp. 11, 14, 21, 42–43; Photos.com, pp. 13, 22, 27.

Cover Photo: Photo courtesy of the Mississippi Development Authority/Division of Tourism.

Cover Description: The Governor's Mansion in downtown Jackson, Mississippi.

Contents

MyReportLinks.com Books
Great Books, Great Links, Great for Research!

MyReportLinks.com Books present the information you need to learn about your report subject. In addition, they show you where to go on the Internet for more information. The pre-evaluated Report Links that back up this book are kept up to date on **www.myreportlinks.com**. With the purchase of a MyReportLinks.com Books title, you and your library gain access to the Report Links that specifically back up that book. The Report Links save hours of research time and link to dozens—even hundreds—of Web sites, source documents, and photos related to your report topic.

Please see "To Our Readers" on the Copyright page for important information about this book, the MyReportLinks.com Books Web site, and the Report Links that back up this book.

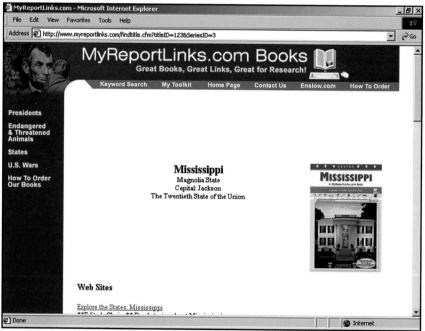

Access:

The Publisher will provide access to the Report Links that back up this book and will try to keep these Report Links up to date on our Web site for three years from the book's first publication date. Please enter **SMS5834** if asked for a password.

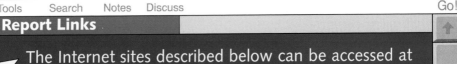
Report Links

The Internet sites described below can be accessed at
http://www.myreportlinks.com

*EDITOR'S CHOICE

▶ **Explore the States: Mississippi**
America's Story from America's Library, a Library of Congress Web site,
tells the story of Mississippi. Here you will learn interesting facts about
the state and its culture.

Link to this Internet site from http://www.myreportlinks.com

*EDITOR'S CHOICE

▶ **Mississippi Department of Archives and History**
At the Mississippi Department of Archives and History you can explore
historic sites, such as the Grand Village of the Natchez Indians,
Historic Jefferson College, and the Winterville Mounds.

Link to this Internet site from http://www.myreportlinks.com

*EDITOR'S CHOICE

▶ **The *World Almanac for Kids Online*: Mississippi**
The *World Almanac for Kids Online* Web site provides essential facts
about Mississippi. Here you will learn about Mississippi's land and
resources, people, government, education system, economy, history, and
much more.

Link to this Internet site from http://www.myreportlinks.com

*EDITOR'S CHOICE

▶ **Nile of the World**
At the National Park Service Web site you can explore the Mississippi
River. Here you will learn about protecting and preserving the lower
Mississippi Delta Region. You will also learn about the Civil War in the
state, the Underground Railroad, and the Delta blues.

Link to this Internet site from http://www.myreportlinks.com

*EDITOR'S CHOICE

▶ **U.S. Census Bureau: Mississippi**
The U.S. Census Bureau Web site provides census data on the state
of Mississippi. Here you will find facts about people, geography, and
business. Click on "Browse more data sets for Mississippi" to learn more.

Link to this Internet site from http://www.myreportlinks.com

*EDITOR'S CHOICE

▶ **Mississippi.gov**
At the Mississippi.gov Web site you will find interesting facts about
Mississippi, including a list of Mississippi's state symbols. You will also
learn about Mississippi's government, tourism, and information about
living and working in the state.

Link to this Internet site from http://www.myreportlinks.com

 The Internet sites described below can be accessed at
http://www.myreportlinks.com

▶ **American Academy of Achievement: Oprah Winfrey**

From the Academy of Achievement Web site you can read this detailed biography of native Mississippian Oprah Winfrey. Learn of her humble beginnings and her rise to fame. You will also find an interview and a brief profile.

Link to this Internet site from http://www.myreportlinks.com

▶ **Bill Strong's Eclectic Mississippi Photo Tour**

Bill Strong, an amateur photographer, offers various tours of Mississippi that include the Gulf Coast, Southern Mississippi, Vicksburg, Mississippi Art, and Morning Stroll.

Link to this Internet site from http://www.myreportlinks.com

▶ **Choctaw Vision**

At the Choctaw Vision Web site you will learn about the history, culture, and tribal economics and enterprises of the Choctaw Indians. Included are a time line, chronology, genealogy, and details of conflicts and wars. You will also find many images.

Link to this Internet site from http://www.myreportlinks.com

▶ **Civil Rights Documentation Project**

The University of Southern Mississippi presents this time line of the civil rights movement in Mississippi. Beginning in the 1950s and lasting until 1970, this Web site presents information about the leaders and activists, boycotts, arrests, and violence during the civil rights movement.

Link to this Internet site from http://www.myreportlinks.com

▶ **Elvis Presley**

At the official Elvis.com Web site you can read all about native Mississippian, and King of Rock 'n' Roll, Elvis Presley. View billboard chart statistics, an overview of his achievements, gold and platinum records, quotes, and many other interesting facts about Elvis.

Link to this Internet site from http://www.myreportlinks.com

▶ **The James D. Hardy Archives**

Learn about the first human lung transplant. It took place at the University of Mississippi Medical Center and was led by Dr. James D. Hardy. Read about Dr. Hardy and his many accomplishments.

Link to this Internet site from http://www.myreportlinks.com

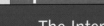
Report Links

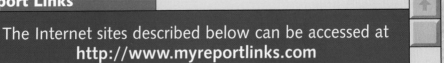
▶ Jefferson Davis Memorial Home Page

Here you will learn about Jefferson Davis, president of the Confederacy. You can also view speeches and inaugural addresses. Images available include Beauvoir, Davis's retirement estate in Biloxi, Mississippi.

Link to this Internet site from http://www.myreportlinks.com

▶ Jimmie Rodgers

Famous Mississippian Jimmie Rodgers is known as the father of country music. Read his biography; view photos; see a list of his songs; and learn about the Jimmie Rodgers Memorial Museum.

Link to this Internet site from http://www.myreportlinks.com

▶ Mark Twain

At this PBS Web site you will learn about Mark Twain, a well-known writer who wrote extensively about the Mississippi River.

Link to this Internet site from http://www.myreportlinks.com

▶ Mississippi History NOW

This online publication from the Mississippi Historical Society is full of historical information. The archives include information on American Indian history, European settlement, general history, African-American history, and more.

Link to this Internet site from http://www.myreportlinks.com

▶ Mississippi Sandhill Crane National Wildlife Refuge

At the Mississippi Sandhill Crane National Wildlife Refuge Web site you can read about the critically endangered Mississippi Sandhill Crane, found nowhere else in the wild but on and adjacent to the refuge.

Link to this Internet site from http://www.myreportlinks.com

▶ Mississippi Sports Hall of Fame and Museum

See all of those who have been inducted into the Mississippi Sports Hall of Fame. View current exhibits, and read about the various features of the complex.

Link to this Internet site from http://www.myreportlinks.com

Report Links

 The Internet sites described below can be accessed at
http://www.myreportlinks.com

▶Muddy Waters

At the official Muddy Waters Web site you can read the biography of native Mississippian and blues legend Muddy Waters. You will also find a discography, and can learn all about Muddy's favorite recipes.

Link to this Internet site from http://www.myreportlinks.com

▶NASA: John C. Stennis Space Center

At the John C. Stennis Space Center Web site you will learn how rocket-propulsion testing is performed for NASA. You can also read the history of the center and view photos.

Link to this Internet site from http://www.myreportlinks.com

▶Natchez Trace Parkway-Mississippi

Learn the history of the Natchez Trace Parkway. Read how the trail winds through three states and has been used by hunters, explorers, and American Indians. Photos are included.

Link to this Internet site from http://www.myreportlinks.com

▶Natureworks: White-tailed Deer

From the Nature Works Web site you can read about the characteristics, classification, behavior, range, habitat, food, and reproduction habits of the white-tailed deer, Mississippi's state land animal. Photos of the white-tailed deer are also included.

Link to this Internet site from http://www.myreportlinks.com

▶Netstate: Mississippi

At the Netstate Web site you will find essential facts about Mississippi. Here you can explore state symbols, geography, maps, and people.

Link to this Internet site from http://www.myreportlinks.com

▶River of Song

This PBS Web site explores life on the Mississippi River. Here you will learn about the musicians who were inspired by the river.

Link to this Internet site from http://www.myreportlinks.com

▶ **Stately Knowledge: Mississippi**

The Internet Public Library Web site provides a "Just the Facts" section about Mississippi. Here you will find population statistics and links to other resources related to Mississippi as well as information about bordering states.

Link to this Internet site from http://www.myreportlinks.com

▶ **Today In History**

The Today In History Web site tells the story of the day that William Faulkner, a famed writer and native Mississippian, was born.

Link to this Internet site from http://www.myreportlinks.com

▶ **USGS Regional Trends of Biological Resources: Mississippi River**

From the United States Geological Survey Web site you will find in-depth information about the Mississippi River. Included are maps, descriptions of the river, its geography, and human development.

Link to this Internet site from http://www.myreportlinks.com

▶ **USGS—The Rivers of Mississippi**

Get information on the river basins of Mississippi, including the Big Black, Coastal Streams, Mississippi, Pascagoula, Pearl, South Independent, Tombigbee, and Yazoo drainage basins. A clickable map is available.

Link to this Internet site from http://www.myreportlinks.com

▶ **Vicksburg National Military Park**

At the National Park Service Web site you can visit the Vicksburg National Military Park located in Vicksburg, Mississippi. Click on "InDepth" to get more information about this historic park.

Link to this Internet site from http://www.myreportlinks.com

▶ **William Tecumseh Sherman**

Read this biography of William Tecumseh Sherman, the general who stormed through Mississippi during the Civil War. A photo of Sherman is included.

Link to this Internet site from http://www.myreportlinks.com

Capital
Jackson

Gained Statehood
December 10, 1817,
the twentieth state

Counties
82

Population
2,844,658*

Bird
Mockingbird

Tree
Magnolia

Flower
Magnolia blossom

Mammal
White-tailed deer or red fox
(land); bottlenosed dolphin
(water)

Fish
Largemouth bass

Insect
Honeybee

Stone
Petrified wood

Song
"Go, Mississippi" (words and
music by Houston Davis)

Motto
Virtute et armis (Latin for "By
valor and arms")

Nickname
Magnolia State

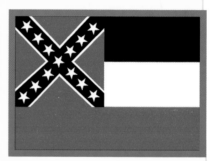

Flag
Three horizontal stripes of blue,
white, and red. The upper left-
hand corner features the blue
crossed stars and bars on a
red background depicting a
Confederate battle flag.

*Population reflects the 2000 census.

Here Along the Great Water

Mississippi and the great river are tied together. The name "Mississippi" comes from an American Indian word meaning "great water" or "big river" or "father of the waters." The state is named for North America's greatest waterway, which forms most of its western border.

Modern-day Mississippi is a changing state. One of the most rural of the fifty states, only about 20 percent of Mississippians live on farms. As they move into small towns and larger cities, their way of life changes.

For example, Mississippi is the largest manufacturer of upholstered furniture in the United States and produces

▲ Two riverboats along the great Mississippi River.

70 percent of the world's supply of pond-raised catfish. The state is home to NASA's John C. Stennis Space Center located in Bay St. Louis on the Gulf Coast. Engines for the United States space shuttles are tested at the complex.

▷ The Crossroads of the South

Mississippi is shaped somewhat like a rectangle standing on its head. Inside the rectangle are 48,430 square miles of land and water, making Mississippi thirty-second of the fifty states in area.[1] In addition to the western boundary of the great river, Mississippi is bordered by Tennessee to the north, Alabama to the east, the Gulf of Mexico to the south, and Louisiana to the south and west.

Mississippi is known as the Magnolia State for the magnolia tree. The white, showy blossoms of the tree are the state flower. The heart of the Magnolia State is Jackson, the capital city. With a population of about four hundred thousand in the metropolitan area—known as Metro Jackson—it is by far the state's largest urban area and the center of government. Jackson retains some of the charm and tranquil look of the days gone by. Known as the heart of the southland, it is a hub of art and architecture and a center for education and health care. The capitol building is modeled after the national capitol in Washington, D.C. This Capital/River Region of Mississippi is known as a strong area for Southern History. That is because "there may be more colorful and quirky museums, major historic sites, and antebellum [before the Civil War] homes per square mile in this region . . . than any place in the United States."[2]

Jackson was founded in 1792 as a trading post on a bluff over the Pearl River. In fact, it was first named

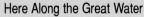

▲ *The magnolia is the state flower. Each blossom has its own unique shape.*

LeFleur's Bluff after French-Canadian trader Louis LeFleur. The town was renamed in 1822 in honor of General Andrew Jackson, who became the seventh president of the United States in 1829.

Growth came slowly to Jackson. Then, General William Tecumseh Sherman and his Union troops stormed through the city three times during the Civil War, destroying property. The Governor's Mansion, built in 1841, was spared. Even at the turn of the twentieth century, Jackson had only about eight thousand people. Then natural gas fields were discovered nearby, railroad transportation increased, and the city grew to be the largest in the state. Long considered a medical pioneer

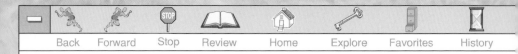

▲ *Located on Ship Island, Fort Massachusetts was a Union stronghold during the Civil War after it was captured from the Confederates in 1861.*

community, Jackson was the site of the world's first lung transplant at the University of Mississippi Medical Center in 1963. Today, Jackson is a major business and distribution center due to its prime location and easy transportation access.

▷ On the Trail

For a quick tour of Mississippi, the visitor might head southeast on azalea-covered Route 49 to Hattiesburg, home of the University of Southern Mississippi. Hattiesburg was settled by William H. Hardy in 1882 and named for his wife, Hattie. The city sits at the edge of the DeSoto National Forest and is the lumber center of the southeastern region. Its population in the year 2000 was listed as 44,779.

Following Route 49 south takes visitors to the towns of Biloxi, Gulfport, and Pascagoula, located on the Gulf Coast. The sister cities of Gulfport and Biloxi are separated by twelve miles of white sand beach. In 2000, Biloxi had a population of 50,644. For generations the city has been home to sailors, fishermen, boat builders, packers and canners, and lately, casino workers. Settled in 1699, its name comes from an American Indian word meaning "broken pot." Not surprisingly, the city's chief industry is seafood.

Gulfport has a population of just over seventy-one thousand and was founded in 1887, also by Captain Hardy. Seafood, lumber, and tourism are its chief industries. All along the Gulf Coast are memorials to the Confederacy and the Deep South. Off the shore of Gulfport is Fort Massachusetts, built just after the Civil War. Pascagoula, located near the Alabama border, is a shipbuilding center that had a 2000 census population of 26,200.

The Pine Region

A drive north from the Gulf Coast along the eastern border leads to Meridian and Columbus in Mississippi's Pine Region. Meridian is the Pine Region's largest city, with a population of 39,968. It was a famous rail link during the Civil War and was the home of Jimmie Rodgers. He was father of country music and the first inductee into the Country Music Hall of Fame. Meridian also hosts the restored Grand Opera House, the only one in the South. Columbus is the birthplace of playwright Tennessee Williams. He wrote about his Mississippi childhood in

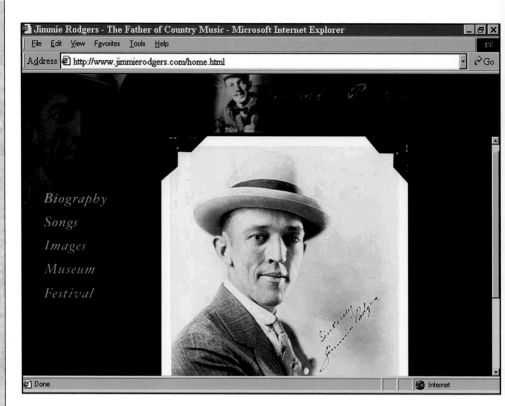

Jimmie Rodgers - The Father of Country Music - Microsoft Internet Explorer

File   Edit   View   Favorites   Tools   Help

Address   http://www.jimmierodgers.com/home.html   Go

Biography
Songs
Images
Museum
Festival

Done   Internet

Mississippi native Jimmie Rodgers was born in 1897. He began his music career as a traveling entertainer when he was thirteen. He sang about cornfields and Southern cities. There is a memorial statue of him in his hometown of Meridian, Mississippi.

some of his most famous works, such as *A Streetcar Named Desire*. The city is also home to Mississippi University for Women, founded in 1884 as the first public college for women in the United States.

Traveling into northeastern Mississippi from Columbus, the road leads to Tupelo, famous as the birthplace of Elvis Presley. This feels like it is a world away from Presley's Graceland mansion in Tennessee. Presley's birthplace had two rooms and cost $180 during the Great Depression of the 1930s, a time of economic hardship.

The city of Tupelo bought it in 1972 with money donated by Presley, and it has been turned into a park and museum for his memorabilia. To the northwest of Tupelo is Oxford, home of another famous American, writer William Faulkner. Beginning with *Sartoris* in 1929, Faulkner invented the Mississippi county of Yoknapatawpha as a setting for his books.

Riverside

Heading due west and then south, the visitor can follow the curves of the Mississippi River as it flows to the Gulf of Mexico. About halfway down the state is Greenville, the largest city in the Delta Region. Its Warfield Point Park boasts one of the best places in the area to view the Mississippi River. It still appears much as it did through the eyes of one of its biggest fans, famed writer Mark Twain. Also known as Samuel Clemens, Twain wrote about life on the Mississippi River in the 1870s and 1880s.

About two thirds of the way down the western border is the historic port city of Vicksburg. More than one million visitors each year come to see the famous Civil War battlefield there.

A short drive to the east brings the visitor back to Jackson and the twenty-first century. That is the charm and reality of Mississippi. It is a state hanging onto much of its past while trying to make a better life for its citizens in a changing world.

Chapter 2

Land and Climate

Mississippi is a small, low-lying state of gentle beauty. The highest point is only 806 feet above sea level on Woodall Mountain in the northeast corner.[1] The land of Mississippi divides into two natural regions, both running north and south. In the west, the flat, narrow stretch of land along the Mississippi River is called the Floodplain. Here is some of the world's richest farmland, thanks to the great river that frequently floods and dumps its rich black soil over the plain. The land along the river between the

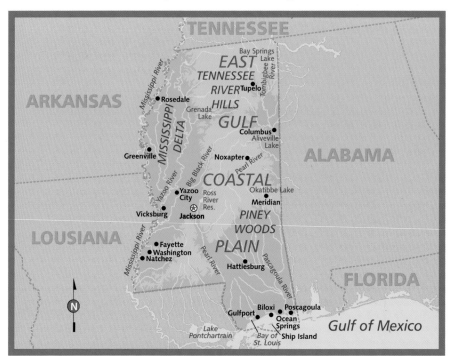

▲ A map of Mississippi.

Yazoo and Mississippi rivers is called the Mississippi Delta. Abundant crops of cotton and soybeans are grown each year in this most important farming region.

The rest of the state is covered by the East Gulf Coastal Plain. Instead of flat farmland, this area contains rolling hills, and much of the land is still undeveloped. The Tennessee River Hills, where Woodall Mountain is located, are located in the northeastern part of the state. The Piney Woods cover the southeastern part of the plain. Pine forests fill the area, which is crisscrossed with streams and low ridges. More than half of the state is forestland. Most of the trees are different varieties of pine, but there are oak, elm, cottonwood, cypress, and poplar as well, in addition to the state tree, the magnolia.

▷ The River

The state of Mississippi has many rivers and streams but none so well known or so important as the river for which it is named. The Mississippi River is one of the twenty longest rivers in the world. From its source in northern Minnesota, it forms most of the state's western border on its way to the Gulf of Mexico, covering 2,340 miles.

After the invention of the steam engine in the nineteenth century, the Mississippi became America's most important waterway. River cities such as Greenville, Vicksburg, and Natchez grew into important shipping centers for the cotton trade. The mighty river is still one of the busiest commercial water routes in the world with shipments of oil and oil products, coal, iron and steel, and chemicals. In addition, the river brings in revenue from tourism. Paddle wheelers that look as they did in the nineteenth century churn past the old restored mansions of the plantation era that line the shore.

Mississippians love and curse the mighty river, because the Mississippi can be a most unruly neighbor. When the river overflows its banks, it deposits rich soil that helps produce healthy and abundant crops. However, when the Mississippi floods, that rich farmland is swept away and so are homes, property, and people.

Attempts to control flooding on the river began as early as 1717. The founding of the city of New Orleans in 1718 made this even more necessary. It was not until 1927, though, that flood control began in earnest. In a catastrophic flood that year, hundreds of people were killed and thousands of acres of forest and farmland were ruined. Congress passed the Flood Control Act in 1928, and in the 1930s, the Army Corps of Engineers began efforts to control the river's floodwaters. The riverbed was dredged to make it deeper and able to carry more water.

The engineers also straightened the river's course. The Mississippi never flows in a straight line but meanders, or curves, across the land. Sometimes the river makes a large loop, almost doubling back upon itself. The engineers shortened the river by cutting across those loops. The part of the river that is cutoff from the rest is called an oxbow lake. Many of them, such as Lee, Moon, and Washington, are located north of Vicksburg. The Mississippi still floods occasionally, but the flood control project helps to keep damage to a minimum.

Two major rivers located in the western part of the state, the Big Black and the Yazoo, flow into the Mississippi. Elsewhere, a network of rivers and streams flows southward to drain into the Gulf of Mexico. The Tombigbee, which originates in the northeast part of the state enters the state of Alabama at Lake Lowndes and drains into the Gulf of Mexico through Mobile Bay.

▲ *Sailing is a very popular pastime along Mississippi's Gulf Coast and in some of the state's larger lakes.*

The Pearl and Pascagoula rivers flow through Mississippi to the Gulf.

Mississippi has only forty-four miles of coastline along the Gulf of Mexico. However, the many bays and coves give it a total shoreline of some 350 miles. A twenty-five-mile-long seawall protects the coast between Biloxi and Point Henderson.

▷ Bayou and Lake Country

Mississippi is a land of bayous, marshy, slow-moving streams that dot the state. Some connect waterways to the Gulf and some connect lakes with rivers in the delta region.

Besides the oxbows, Mississippi has many lakes that are man-made reservoirs. Ross Barnett Lake reservoir, built in the 1960s to hold thirty-three thousand acres of water on the Pearl River, supplies the city of Jackson.[2]

Animal Life

Where once the buffalo and cougar roamed, Mississippi is a land of smaller animals such as foxes, opossums, squirrels, and the white-tailed deer. With so much undeveloped land, the state is a hunting and fishing paradise. Conservation efforts are trying to keep the deer from disappearing. Quail, duck, and wild turkey are plentiful, and swampy areas are full of alligators and water moccasins. The state has many varieties of birds, some of them

▲ *Mississippi's sandhill crane is an endangered subspecies found nowhere else in the world. They are typically gray in color and have a wingspan of six feet.*

endangered, such as the ivory-billed woodpecker, the sandhill crane, and the brown pelican.

Mississippi is famous for its catfish, but crabs, shrimp, oysters, mackerel, bass, and speckled trout also are found in abundance.

The Climate

A land of the Deep South, Mississippi's climate can best be described as hot. In the southeast, the temperature is often higher than 100°F throughout July and August. The winters are short and the summers long. Farmers take advantage of the 250 or more days of growing season each year. The average temperature statewide for July is about 80°F; in January about 46°F. It always seems hotter in summer because of the generally high humidity.

About fifty inches of rain fall yearly in the northwest, and about sixty-five inches in the southeast. It is rare, but sometimes snow and sleet cover the ground in the northern part of the state.

Mississippi is in a tornado path. It ranks fifth in the United States in the number of these funnel-shaped storms that often reach the ground with deadly consequences. One of the worst tornadoes occurred in Natchez in 1840. It killed 317 people and sank steamboats on the Mississippi River. In 1936, a twister hit Tupelo and killed 216 people. Between 1950 and 1995 over one thousand tornadoes hit the state, killing 387 people.[3]

Mississippi receives fierce hurricanes, too, from the Gulf of Mexico. One of the worst was Camille, which hit the state in 1969. Camille's winds reached an amazing two hundred plus miles per hour. Over a two-day period, 256 people were killed, and more than 40,000 homes were destroyed.

Chapter 3

The People and Their Work

The people of Mississippi are predominately black and white Americans—about 61 percent white, 36 percent black. A small population of American Indians lives in the east central section of the state. A number of Chinese Americans live in the Delta region, and there is a community of Southeast Asians along the coastal area. In 2000, there were 2,844,658 people who called Mississippi home.

Since the beginning of its history, Mississippi has been divided along racial lines. Although, slow but constant changes have occurred since the bitter days of the civil rights struggles of the mid-1900s. The people of Mississippi are finding ways to live and work together. This is how the state keeps its reputation as the Hospitality State.

One of the enduring problems between races in Mississippi has been the state flag. It carries the "stars and crossed bars," the battle flag symbol of the Confederate States of America used during the Civil War. White Mississippians regard the old symbol as part of their past; black Mississippians regard it as a reminder of slavery and injustice. The people became so agitated over the issue that they voted in a referendum on April 17, 2001. The result was 488,630 to 267,812 to keep the Mississippi flag as it is.[1]

▷ Music

One aspect of life that unites all Mississippians is music. The state has a rich musical history. It is the birthplace of

Elvis Presley, who was born in Tupelo on January 8, 1935. Presley's father built their small home with $180 he borrowed for materials.[2] Presley lived there until the family moved to Memphis, Tennessee, when he was thirteen.

Most of all, Mississippi is known as the "birthplace of the blues." The blues began in the Delta region near the beginning of the twentieth century. Blues songs are brooding, sometimes painful tunes that came from the hearts of descendants of slaves and poor African-American sharecroppers. African influences are evident in its tones. By the second half of the century, the development of popular music in the United States had been influenced strongly by the Mississippi Delta blues. The blues are

Elvis Presley is known as "The King of Rock 'n' Roll." In his career, he sold over one billion records and starred in thirty-three successful films.

performed in a speech like pattern with a rhythmic guitar playing along. Some of its gifted originators were Charley Patton, Willie Brown, Eddie "Son" House, Robert Johnson, and Johnny Shines.

▷ Religion

Mississippi is located in what some call the Bible Belt, and has more churches per person than any other state. A majority of Mississippians are Protestants—mostly Baptist and United Methodist. Roman Catholic and Jewish populations are centered mainly in the urban areas.

Especially for African Americans, churches in Mississippi were places of peace and refuge during the days of slavery and later during the civil rights movement. Unfortunately, hate groups such as the Ku Klux Klan sometimes used African-American churches as targets for bombings or burnings.

▷ Mississippi at Work

Say the words "Mississippi's economy" and many people think of cotton. For decades, cotton was the most important crop in what was an agricultural state. Cotton is still important—Mississippi is the nation's third largest cotton producer after Texas and California—but the state has become less dependent on agriculture overall. Profits from farming provide only about 3 percent of the state's gross annual product. One area on the rise is catfish farming. Mississippi produces the most commercial catfish in the nation. Acres of old plantation fields have been converted into hatcheries throughout the Delta region.

Modern Mississippi is making strides in service industries. These include wholesale and retail sales, banking and insurance, government services, health care,

▲ Cotton grows abundantly in warm climates. It is a major industry in Mississippi. In 1997, the cotton industry employed nearly thirty thousand Mississippians. In 2002, cotton crops covered 1.18 million acres of the state.

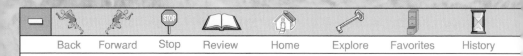

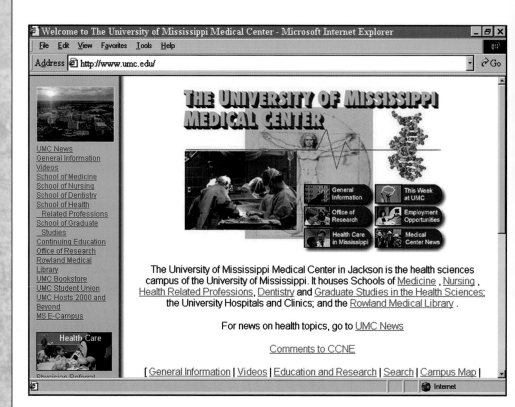

▲ *Ole Miss was granted the University of Mississippi Medical Center in 1950. The center opened in 1955. In 1963, the world's first lung transplant operation was performed there.*

and public education. Shipbuilding has become a part of the state's economy, with shipyards lining the Gulf Coast. Forestry and the manufacturing of wood products is on the rise. Tourism is an increasingly important source of income. Civil War historic sites bring in many visitors as, increasingly, do the casinos that now dot the Mississippi River.

Mississippi has long suffered from poor economic growth. Although its workforce is ample, its workers are among the lowest paid in the nation. The per capita income, which measures annual income earned by each person, was $20,993 as reported by the census of 2000. That figure was the lowest among the fifty states. Since late in the twentieth century, Mississippi's governors have pledged to bring more industry to the state, improve the training of its workforce, and boast the quality of its public education.

▷ Education

A poor education system has long plagued the public schools of the Magnolia State. Mississippi has a high school graduation rate of 60 percent, the fifth-lowest in the nation. Teachers' salaries are well below the national average, and classroom resources are limited. Yet, the state has been making concentrated efforts to improve the quality of education since the 1980s with passage of the Education Reform Act. This law mandates that children between ages six and fourteen must attend school. That law had been repealed in 1956 to avoid integrating the public schools as ordered by the federal government. School desegregation statewide did not begin until 1970, but now all of the state's public schools are desegregated.

Though the public school's may have needed improvement, Mississippi has been proud of its institutions of higher learning. One of the first in the country, Jefferson College, was established in 1802. The University of Mississippi at Oxford was opened in 1848. It is known as "Ole Miss."

Mississippi College, the oldest college in Mississippi, began in Clinton in 1826. Mississippi State, located in Starkville, contains a first-rate agricultural research facility. The country's first college to grant degrees to women was

▲ *Mississippi College is the oldest institution of higher learning in the state. This image shows the Provine Chapel in the 1930s.*

Whitworth College. It began as the Elizabeth Female Academy in 1818. The school is now known as the Mississippi School of Arts. In addition to its private and public institutions, there are more than one hundred technical/vocational schools and junior/community colleges in the state.

Jackson: How the Government Runs

The capital city of Jackson is the seat of state government for Mississippi. Like the federal government in Washington, D.C., Mississippi operates under a constitution. The constitution was adopted in 1890. Three earlier constitutions were adopted in 1817, 1832, and 1869. The constitution can be amended by a majority of voters in a general election or by constitutional convention.

▶ Branches of Government

Also like the federal government, Mississippi's government has three branches: executive, legislative, and judicial. The executive branch is led by the governor, who is elected for a four-year term. Until 1988, the governor could not serve consecutive terms. This weakened executive power.

The main duties of the governor are to develop state policies concerning economics, education, and law enforcement, and to prepare the state budget. In addition, the governor accepts or rejects bills that have been passed by the state legislature. Mississippi's governor lives in a mansion built in 1841 and modeled after the White House.

The legislative branch is the lawmaking body of the state. Mississippi's legislature is bicameral. That means that it has two parts: a senate of 52 members and a house of representatives with 122 members. The members are elected to four-year terms and meet for ninety days each year except in the year after which a governor is elected. In those years, the legislature meets for 125 days.

The building in which the legislature meets is the state

capitol in Jackson, built in 1903 on the site of an old state prison. Its huge dome is topped by a gold-leafed copper eagle with a wingspan of fifteen feet. From 1839 until 1903, government activity was conducted in the Old Capitol, which was restored during 1959–61 and is now a National Historic Landmark. The Old Capitol Museum boasts extensive memorabilia on Jefferson Davis, the president of the Confederacy. It was in that building in 1861 that Mississippi became the second state to secede from the Union, igniting the Civil War. The Old Capitol is also the site of the Mississippi State Historical Museum.[1]

The legislature has great powers. It makes laws,

▲ Mississippi has had three state capitol buildings. The third and current state capitol building, completed in 1903, was built because the Old Capitol building was too small to house the growing government.

approves the state budget, and levies taxes. The legislature oversees the whole network of administrative business.

Mississippi's judicial system interprets the laws passed by the legislature. The highest court is the supreme court of nine members who serve eight-year terms.

The lowest court is the justice court, which handles most misdemeanors and fines. The state has two types of trial courts—circuit courts that hear civil and criminal cases, and chancery courts that hear only civil cases. Other courts include municipal, justice, and family courts for which all justices serve four-year terms.

▷ Politics

For all practical purposes, between 1876 and 1944, the Democratic Party was the only political party in the state. Mississippians voted for Democratic candidates in every major local, state, and national election during

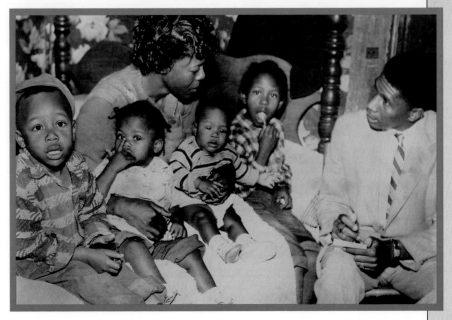

▲ *NAACP activist Medgar Evers (right) was killed on June 12, 1963.*

that period. The state was considered a easy victory for the Democratic Party.

The struggle for civil rights in the mid-twentieth century began to change the political picture. When the national Democratic Party openly supported desegregation and civil rights, white Mississippians began to turn away. After the Civil Rights Act of 1964 and the Voting Rights Act of 1965, more and more African Americans were able to join the voting ranks. In 1969, Charles Evers was elected mayor of Fayette, Mississippi. He became the first African-American mayor in Mississippi since the Reconstruction period

Thad Cochran was elected to the Senate in 1978. He was the first Republican to be elected to the U.S. Senate from Mississippi in over one hundred years.

after the Civil War. His brother, Medgar Evers had been a well-known civil rights activist. Medgar Evers was shot and killed in Jackson, in 1963.

For a time, there were two Democratic parties in the state. One was predominantly African American and allied with the more liberal National Party. The other was conservative, favoring the past. Eventually the two reunited, but conservative Mississippians were still dissatisfied. In the 1970s, Mississippians voted more and more for Republican candidates. In 1978, Thad Cochran, the first Republican senator from Mississippi since the Civil War, went to Congress, followed by Senator Trent Lott in 1989. In 1992, Kirk Fordice became the state's first Republican governor since 1876.

The people of Mississippi have a long history of being outspoken. This includes the racist secret activities of the Ku Klux Klan and their violent protests against civil rights legislation in the 1950s and 1960s. In 1954, the U.S. Supreme Court declared segregation in public schools to be against the law, but Mississippi's Senator James O. Eastland told his people not to obey the decision. Hundreds of African Americans in the state were jailed for violating segregation laws or attempting to desegregate public eating places. In 1962, Governor Ross Barnett defied the U.S. attorney general by refusing to admit an African-American student, James Meredith, to the University of Mississippi. After a riot, Meredith was accepted, and the color barrier in the state of Mississippi was broken.

By 2003, about 13 percent of the enrollment at Ole Miss was African American. In the spring of 2002, Joseph Meredith, the son of James, quietly graduated from the university with a doctorate in business administration.[2]

State History

Thousands of years ago, nomadic peoples roamed the land that is now Mississippi. They are known as Mound Builders because of the heaps of earth they erected in the center of their villages. Early in the sixteenth century, Americans Indians—mainly Choctaw in the central area, Natchez in the southwest, and Chickasaw in the north

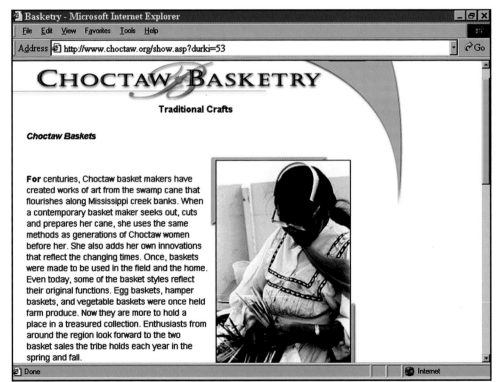

Basketry - Microsoft Internet Explorer

File Edit View Favorites Tools Help

Address http://www.choctaw.org/show.asp?durki=53

CHOCTAW BASKETRY

Traditional Crafts

Choctaw Baskets

For centuries, Choctaw basket makers have created works of art from the swamp cane that flourishes along Mississippi creek banks. When a contemporary basket maker seeks out, cuts and prepares her cane, she uses the same methods as generations of Choctaw women before her. She also adds her own innovations that reflect the changing times. Once, baskets were made to be used in the field and the home. Even today, some of the basket styles reflect their original functions. Egg baskets, hamper baskets, and vegetable baskets were once held farm produce. Now they are more to hold a place in a treasured collection. Enthusiasts from around the region look forward to the two basket sales the tribe holds each year in the spring and fall.

Done   Internet

▲ Choctaw basket makers weave their baskets out of swamp cane found along Mississippi creek banks. These baskets have been made for centuries and were originally used in both the field and home. Now they are more of an art form.

and east—lived in the area. The Choctaw numbered about twenty thousand and lived in the southern and central parts of the state. They trace their history to Nanih Waiya, a sacred hill located near present-day Noxapter.[1] About 4,500 of the Natchez tribe lived in the southwest and about 5,000 Chickasaw in the northeast. The French garrison at Fort Rosalie (now the city of Natchez) virtually killed all the Natchez during 1729–31. The other two tribes were eventually moved to reservations in the Oklahoma Territory in the 1830s.

▷ Exploration

In the winter of 1540, Hernando de Soto, a Spanish explorer and conquistador, led a large expedition into what is now Mississippi and wintered along the Pontotoc River. He reached the mighty river the following spring. However, because he found no gold or silver in the region, he did not explore farther.

It was more than a century later that a French-Canadian, Pierre Le Moyne, Sieur d'Iberville, explored the northern coast of the Gulf of Mexico. He became the third European explorer to reach the mouth of the Mississippi, in 1699. He later built Fort Maurepas (now Ocean Springs, Mississippi) on Biloxi Bay. He established a second fort, La Boulaye, near present-day New Orleans. In 1673, Father Jacques Marquette, a Jesuit priest, and Louis Joliet, a fur trapper, traveled to where the Arkansas River joins the Mississippi River at present-day Rosedale. Nine years later, René-Robert Cavelier, Sieur de La Salle, explored the river from Canada down to the Gulf Coast. He claimed all the region for France and named the huge territory Louisiana in honor of King Louis XIV. In 1719, the first black slaves were brought to the area from West

Africa. They worked in the rice and tobacco fields of the French colonists.

When the French and Indian War ended in 1763, France gave up its possessions on the eastern side of the lower Mississippi Valley, with the exception of New Orleans, to Great Britain. Great Britain split its new possessions into two regions. What is now northern Mississippi became part of the colony of Georgia. Southern Mississippi joined the province of West Florida.

▷ The Revolution and the Territory

In 1775, the American Revolution began as the English colonies fought for independence from Great Britain. Georgia's settlers were mainly in favor of the colonists. West Florida stood behind Great Britain. While the British were fighting elsewhere, in 1781, Spain took over West Florida without opposition.

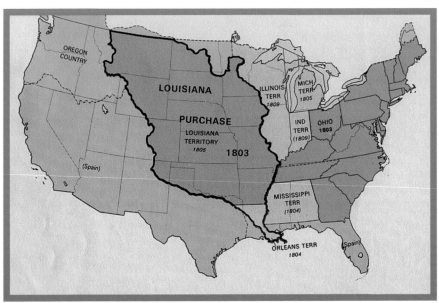

▲ A map of territorial growth in the United States as the country appeared in 1810.

At the end of the war, the American colonies gained their independence, and the British officially gave West Florida to Spain. The boundary between the new United States of America and Spanish West Florida was fixed at the 31st parallel, now part of the border between Mississippi and Louisiana. In 1819, all of Spanish West Florida would become part of the United States.

In 1798, the U.S. Congress created the Mississippi Territory. It extended from the Mississippi River to the Chattahoochee rivers on the Georgia border, and from the mouth of the Yazoo River south to the 31st parallel. In 1804, the northern border of the territory was extended to the border of Tennessee. Natchez was the first capital of the territory.

Statehood

In 1803, the United States bought the vast Louisiana Territory from France. Now the Mississippi River was open to commerce. In 1817, part of the territory became Mississippi, the twentieth state in the Union.

At a constitutional convention in the village of Washington, Mississippi, David Holmes was selected as the state's first governor on October 17, 1817. Natchez was named the state capital. About twenty-five thousand whites and twenty-three thousand black slaves lived in the state. Although they were not counted in the census, the population also included about thirty-five thousand American Indians. The state capital was moved to Jackson in 1822.

The first half of the nineteenth century was a time of cotton growing. Steamboat traffic on the river in Mississippi was high. American Indians were moved out of the state, but the slave population was growing.

Generally, slaves were part of the large plantations and not common among the small landowners.

The Civil War

Slavery, however, was the main reason for the growing rift between Northern and Southern states, which finally led to the Civil War (1861–65). The first fight of the war on Mississippi soil was the Battle of Shiloh, waged on April 6, 1862. Although the South was victorious, both sides were shocked at the terrible cost. More than one hundred thousand men fought on a field next to Shiloh, a small, whitewashed church. More than thirteen thousand were

Photo Album: Northeast View, National Cemetery - Microsoft Internet Explorer

File   Edit   View   Favorites   Tools   Help

Address http://www.nps.gov/vick/scenic/h_natcem/pa_ne.htm

Done   Internet

▲ *Vicksburg National Cemetery is known for having the largest number of Civil War graves. It is also the resting place of veterans from the Spanish-American War, both World Wars, and the Korean War.*

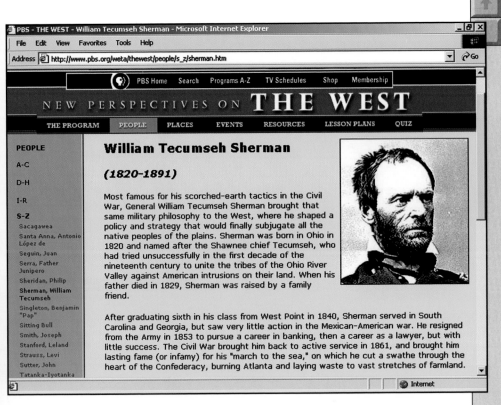

PBS - THE WEST - William Tecumseh Sherman - Microsoft Internet Explorer

File   Edit   View   Favorites   Tools   Help

Address   http://www.pbs.org/weta/thewest/people/s_z/sherman.htm   Go

PBS Home   Search   Programs A-Z   TV Schedules   Shop   Membership

NEW PERSPECTIVES ON THE WEST

THE PROGRAM   PEOPLE   PLACES   EVENTS   RESOURCES   LESSON PLANS   QUIZ

PEOPLE

A-C

D-H

I-R

S-Z
Sacagawea
Santa Anna, Antonio López de
Seguin, Juan
Serra, Father Junipero
Sheridan, Philip
Sherman, William Tecumseh
Singleton, Benjamin "Pap"
Sitting Bull
Smith, Joseph
Stanford, Leland
Strauss, Levi
Sutter, John
Tatanka-Iyotanka

William Tecumseh Sherman

(1820–1891)

Most famous for his scorched-earth tactics in the Civil War, General William Tecumseh Sherman brought that same military philosophy to the West, where he shaped a policy and strategy that would finally subjugate all the native peoples of the plains. Sherman was born in Ohio in 1820 and named after the Shawnee chief Tecumseh, who had tried unsuccessfully in the first decade of the nineteenth century to unite the tribes of the Ohio River Valley against American intrusions on their land. When his father died in 1829, Sherman was raised by a family friend.

After graduating sixth in his class from West Point in 1840, Sherman served in South Carolina and Georgia, but saw very little action in the Mexican-American war. He resigned from the Army in 1853 to pursue a career in banking, then a career as a lawyer, but with little success. The Civil War brought him back to active service in 1861, and brought him lasting fame (or infamy) for his "march to the sea," on which he cut a swathe through the heart of the Confederacy, burning Atlanta and laying waste to vast stretches of farmland.

Internet

Union General William Tecumseh Sherman aided Ulysses Grant at the Battle of Vicksburg, Mississippi, in 1863. This siege lasted from March 29 to July 4, and resulted in the Confederacy surrendering control of the Mississippi River.

dead, missing, or wounded for the North and nearly eleven thousand for the South.[2]

Although there was fierce fighting in many areas in Mississippi during the war, the most important action was at Vicksburg in 1863. On a high bluff over the great river, a siege lasted from May 18 to July 4. In the end, General Ulysses S. Grant and the Union Army triumphed, and the victory cut the Confederacy in two. The town was so angered that it refused to celebrate another Fourth of July until 1944. Many historic sites remain from the siege,

▲ *Jackson, the state capital, is also Mississippi's largest city.*

such as the restored Duff Green Mansion, "constructed by skilled slave labor and a hospital for Confederate and Union soldiers during the Civil War."[3]

▶ The Long Aftermath

After victory by the Union in 1865, Mississippi lay in economic ruin. The state immediately passed "black codes," which took away the rights given to the freed slaves in the Fourteenth Amendment. The state grappled with the consequences as the white majority would not accept equal treatment under the law. Mississippi, like other states that had seceded, was placed under military law in 1869.

The state was not allowed to rejoin the Union until 1870 after a new constitution promised free public education, and a repeal of the black codes. African Americans became part of the new legislature in the state.

The period of Reconstruction, intended to help rebuild the South after the war, was largely a failure. Those who genuinely wanted to aid Reconstruction eventually lost out to those seeking their own profits. Dissatisfaction led to new legislation in Mississippi, which brought back white supremacy. Hate groups formed, such as the Ku Klux Klan. Their members hid their identities behind hoods and lynched African

Americans. Jim Crow laws enforced strict segregation of the races. A new constitution in 1890 stripped African Americans of their civil rights.

▷ Civil Rights

A separation of the races and a lack of civil rights plagued the state of Mississippi in the first half of the twentieth century. The events following World War II, though, brought about a revolution of a new kind. First came the jolting U.S. Supreme Court decision in 1954 that declared segregated schools illegal. The case was known as *Brown* v. *Board of Education*. For years, Mississippi and other Southern states fought the ruling. Federal troops had to be sent in to escort African-American students into public schools. Then came the fight at Ole Miss over acceptance of James Meredith in 1962. The worst violence of all erupted in 1964. Three young civil rights workers were murdered in Mississippi by members of the Ku Klux Klan. It was this atrocity that shocked the nation and convinced many Mississippians that resistance was no longer worth the price. These events inspired the chilling movie *Mississippi Burning* released in 1988.

The scars are deep, bigotry remains, and the past is not easily forgotten. There have been profound changes, as well. There are no longer public fights about African-American admittance to Ole Miss; the state's school system is integrated fully; African Americans and whites eat in the same restaurants and attend the same theaters. Mississippians are trying to work together for economic growth and harmony in the twenty-first century.

Chapter Notes

Chapter 1. Here Along the Great Water

1. Borgna Brunner, ed., *Time Almanac 2003* (Boston: Information Please, 2002), p. 177.

2. *Mississippi: The Official Tour Guide*, Mississippi Tourism Association, 2002.

Chapter 2. Land and Climate

1. Borgna Brunner, ed., *Time Almanac 2003* (Boston: Information Please, 2002), p. 503.

2. Ross Barnett Reservoir.org, "Welcome to the Pearl River Valley Water Supply District," *Barnett Reservoir*, 2001, <http://www.rossbarnettreservoir.org/> (April 29, 2003).

3. Disaster Center, "Mississippi Tornadoes," *The Disaster Center Tornado Page*, n.d., <http://www.disastercenter.com/miss/tornado.html> (April 29, 2003).

Chapter 3. The People and Their Work

1. Cable News Network, "Mississippi will retain its 107-year-old flag," *Insidepolitics*, April 18, 2001, <www.cnn.com/2001/ALLPOLITICS/04/18/mississippi.flag/index.html> (April 28, 2003).

2. "Attractions," *Tupelo: All American City*, n.d., <http://ci.tupelo.ms.us/attractions.html> (April 28, 2003).

Chapter 4. Jackson: How the Government Runs

1. Stephen Hawkins, "Jackson reflects mix of past struggles and today's progress," October 19, 1999, <http://www.usatoday.com/travel/vacations/1999/t0615ms.htm> (April 28, 2003).

2. David M. Halbfinger, "40 Years After Infamy, Ole Miss Looks to Reflect and Heal," *New York Times*, September 27, 2002, p. A1.

Chapter 5. State History

1. Choctaw Nation of Oklahoma, "Choctaw Nation History," *Choctaw Nation of Oklahoma*, 2002, <http://www.choctawnation.com/content.php?mmi_id=4&smill_id=&page=71> (April 28, 2003).

2. Mary Beth Norton, David M. Katzman, Paul E. Escott, et. al, A *People & A Nation: A History of the United States Volume I: To 1877* (Boston: Houghton Mifflin Company, 1990), p. 403.

3. Scenario Partner Publications, "Vicksburg, Warren County," *Mississippi Scenario Magazine*, 1998–2003, <http://scenariousa.com/ms/warren/vicksburg.html> (April 28, 2003).

Further Reading

Archer, Jules. *A House Divided: The Lives of Ulysses S. Grant & Robert E. Lee.* Madison, Wisc.: Turtleback Books, 1997.

Bramwell, Martyn. *Rivers and Lakes.* New York: Watts, 1994.

Davis, Charles. *Mississippi.* Chicago: Children's Press, 1999.

Fireside, Harvey. *The "Mississippi Burning" Civil Rights Murder Conspiracy Trial.* Berkeley Heights, N.J.: Enslow Publishers, Inc., 2002.

Foran, Jill. *A Guide to Mississippi.* Mankato, Minn.: Weigl Publishers, Inc., 2000.

Fradin, Dennis. *Mississippi: From Sea to Shining Sea.* Chicago: Children's Press, 1995.

Kummer, Patricia K. *Mississippi: One Nation.* Minnetonka, Minn.: Capstone Press, Incorporated, 2003.

Lester, Julius. *To Be a Slave,* rev. ed. New York: Dial, 1998.

Sanford, William R. *The Natchez Trace Historic Trail in American History.* Berkeley Heights, N.J.: Enslow Publishers, Inc., 2001.

Shirley, David. *Mississippi.* Tarrytown, N.Y.: Marshall Cavendish Corp., 1999.

Siebert, Diane. *Mississippi.* New York: HarperCollins Children's Book Group, 2001.